To my family for all their love and support, to teachers who care and to the children who need it most.

Also available by Ian Moore:

Illustrated Children's Poetry Book
Poems, Beans and Chips! (illustrated by Mike Dicey)
ISBN: 978-0-9567314-0-1

Short Stories for Children
A Funny Pair of Shorts (An Omnibus of Grandog and Escaping Ellen)
ISBN: 978-0-9567314-2-5

eBooks
Poems, Beans and Chips!
Poems, Beans and Chips! presents *Poems for SEAL, PSHCE and Assemblies*
Escaping Ellen
Grandog

Praise for *Poems, Beans and Chips!*
"A fantastic little book that has supported my planning and teaching of a year 3 poetry topic. The children loved the poems as well."

'Entertaining and amusing book of poems for all ages. Fun poems and delightful sketches are just right for any age. Encourages youngsters to read and have a go at writing their own poems!'

'If you are doing Language Play with children you couldn't do better than use this as a resource. It appeals to all ages.'

'As a mum, I have had great fun sharing these poems with my 8 year old at home - she knows most of them off by heart & often asks for one (or two!) after a story, before she goes to sleep. Her favourite is 'Biscuit Girl'! We both enjoy the fun colour illustrations and clear layout. As a teacher, I have successfully used the poems for word play, alliteration and so on in Literacy and also some poems lend themselves well to SEAL themes. 'Anger' works brilliantly as a springboard into discussing ways of controlling our tempers. Children love to give a group performance of this poem - perhaps as a whole class split into the two sides; everyone joins in the chorus, muttering it 'under their breath'! This can be very effective and can then lead into the children colour-coding a copy of the poem to show signs of external and internal anger. If you're a teacher, try it!'

Contents

Introduction

Welcome to this paperback edition of '*Poems for SEAL*, PSHCE** and Assemblies*', which was originally published as an eBook for teachers of children aged seven to thirteen. Awareness of the need to champion children's mental health difficulties, and the importance of safeguarding and prioritising children's welfare, has grown in recent years, and rightly so. This book has been published to help with that in whatever way it can. I have received positive feedback about how these poems have been used by teachers and embraced by children in giving them insights into others' needs, understanding their own, letting children know that they are not alone, and allowing a safe media for exploring challenging emotions and situations.

This book includes accessible poems on a whole range of themes and topics important to children today; ranging from anti-bullying messages (Alone, Bullied), to being in care and having a parent in prison (New Girl), the loss of a pet (Goodbye) and living with Autism (Old Professor Me) through to embarrassment and personal hygiene (Yesterday's Socks). There is a strong focus on recognising and celebrating individual differences, whether they relate to culture, ethnicity, religion, disability or additional needs.

Ian Moore
www.moorethanwords.co.uk

* Social and Emotional Aspects of Learning
** Personal, Social, Health and Citizenship Education

Different

I can't eat what you eat,
I can't play down your street.
Mostly – yeah, that's fine,
But just from time to time...
I wish I looked the same,
Knew how to dance and aim.
Ate all the food that you eat,
Was allowed to play down your street.

Alone

Alone,	alone;	sitting,	alone.
Alone,	alone;	slumped here,	alone.
Alone,	alone;	in my,	own home.
Alone,	alone;	no-one,	to phone.
Alone,	alone;	waiting,	alone.
Alone,	alone;	crying,	alone.

Bullied

The first thing,
The VERY first thing...
That I do
Each lunchtime
Is run.

The next thing,
The VERY next thing...
That I do
Each lunchtime
Is hide.

New Girl

New girl, they say.
New girl, each day.

Asking all about my Mum,
About the place I'm really from.

New girl, they say.
New girl, each day.

Shoved about from place to place,
In each new school a brand new face.

New girl, they say.
New girl, each day.

Strangers say this new one's home,
While mum sits in that cell alone.

War

When I was four,
War
Was exciting.
Fighting!
Guns and gangs,
Bang Bang Bang...
Tearing round town being tyrants.

Now I'm more,
War
Is frightening.
Fighting.
Guns and gangs,
Bang Bang Bang...
Tearing up towns with its violence.

Yesterday's Socks

Over-slept, quick - get dressed!
    Yesterday's socks.
Icky, sticky...slightly damp.
    Yesterday's socks.
Dash downstairs, toast and cheese,
    Yesterday's socks.

Rush to school, register,
    Yesterday's socks.
Drama now, shoes off please!'
    Yesterday's socks.
'Porr, wossthat? It really stinks!'
    Yesterday's socks.

Playtime comes, kick-about,
    Yesterday's socks.
Running, sweating, lunchtime sun,
    Yesterday's socks.
Cook indoors, windows shut,
    Yesterday's socks.

Hide and seek, in the sun,
    Yesterday's socks.
Round hers for tea, finally,
    Yesterday's socks.
'The carpet's new, shoes off please!'
    Yesterday's socks.

Now she's gagging, eyes bulge wide,
    Yesterday's socks.
Mum's gone out, I'm stuck here.
    Yesterday's socks.
She's still staring, I'm still wearing
    Yesterday's socks.

<u>School Disco</u>

So it's
hula hoop...pooper scoop...Cup-a-Soup
Ready for tonight!

I'm in
hot pursuit...planned my route...he's so cute!
Dance with him tonight!

But he's
penalty shoot...golden boot...what-a-hoot!
With the boys tonight!

<u>I don't, I can't</u>

I don't know,
What I don't know.
But finding out will help me grow.

I can't see,
What I can't see.
Who do you see when you see me?

Wishing

I know you bite your toenails,
And you must go to the loo.
But even so I waste each day,
Just wishing I was you.

Is It True?

My favourite shape's a circle,
I so love eating snow.
Is it true that horse manure helps scented flowers grow?

My favourite colour's purple,
I can't stand touching chalk.
Is it true that some babies can run before they walk?

My favourite limb's my left leg.
I can't speak Japanese.
Is it true that burger bars cause chopping down of trees?

My Sister's Having A Baby

My sister's having a baby.
Maybe
They'll get the room next to mine.
That would be fine,
With me but not mum.
All grizzly and glum...
Says sis is too young.
Way, way too young.
But
My sister's having a baby,
And just maybe
They'll get the room next to mine.

Where Was You Lenny?

Where was you Lenny,
My Brother, last night?
When half of the high street slipped out of the light?

Where was you Lenny,
Big Brother, oh please?
When the place that protects me was brought to its knees?

Where was you Lenny,
Our Lenny, this morn?
As that copper from Cleethorpes lay tattered and torn?

Sick, Sick Society

Sick, sick society?
Set in the rot!
Heinous hoodies, arson and plot.

Sick, sick society?
Benefits blamed!
Will a problem be solved when he's Named and he's Shamed?

Cyber-Buddying

I text you, you text me,
We're best friends as friends should be.
With a great big smiley and a kiss from me to you...
We're just best friends through and through.

I text you, you text me,
Night on night so mis'rably,
With a great big sad-face and a pic from me to you...
The one you hate, you're on the loo.

I text him, he texts her,
Words and pics that cause a stir
With a great big hassle that was caused by me and you...
And all I feel is 'I miss you'.

<u>Goodbye</u>

Farewell
Mud-roller, squirrel-chaser
Tail-wagger, rat-racer
Au revoir

Sleep well
Bed-warmer, meat-nicker
Sock-chewer, face-licker
Goodbye

Old Professor Me

My ears they hear too much,
    My clothes all itch to touch.

I don't get what you say,
    So on my own I play.

That does, though, make me calm,
    Like when I flap my arm.

You cringe at how I act,
    But I won't forget one fact.

Old Professor Me,
    King of ICT.

I'm really rather good,
    At not being understood.

I'd rather not have choice,
    Use keyboard as my voice.

Eat food that's mainly yellow,
    And hope with age I'll mellow.

But now I just hate change,
    And when you rearrange.

My ears they hear too much,
    My clothes all itch to touch.

<u>Trapped</u>

Trapped
In my skin
Letting no-one
In

Trapped
In my mind
Letting no-one
Find

Trapped
In my head
Wishing I was
Dead

Caring, I mean, a LOT

My brother's up all night,
I mean – ALL night!
It makes mum cry.
A lot.
And his roaring and her crying make me
Tired.

My brother's helped at school,
I mean – just LOADS!
It makes him smile.
A lot.
But his roaring and mum's crying leave me
Behind.

My brother's my best friend,
I mean – the BEST!
Me makes me smile.
A lot,
But I wish more help came to young
Carers.

Vile Valentine

Vile vile Valentine,
    Slippy sloppy kiss.
Hearts and bows and scented rose...
    Boo!
    Yuck!
    Hiss!

Vile vile Valentine,
    Sign it with a kiss.
Hearts-in-shards through lack of cards...
    Boo!
    Yuck!
    Hiss!

Dress me up as Frankenstein,
    Valentine's Day missed.
No girls or guys or pink surprise...
    Oo!
    Lush!
    Bliss!

Leavers' Poem

(The name of your school can be inserted instead of 'Primary' below.)

One day was your first day,
Soon now comes your last,
As you say 'ta-rah!' to Primary,
Your Now becomes your Past.

You're
  Leaving
  Grieving
  Nose-on-sleeving.

But...
  Although a tear may be shed,
  Along the way, it must be said...

You had...
  Sand and water, playdough, bricks,
  Learning three and three makes six.
  Rock hard pizza, toilet roll,
  'Off those wall-bars!', score a goal!
  Sportsmad, 'Good lad!', need-the-loo,
  Pirates, Tudors, World War 2.

One day was your first day,
Soon now comes your last,
As you say 'ta-rah!' to Primary,
Your Now becomes your Past.

Something To Say

It started off at school
     as we walked up to the hall,
I was feeling so unwell
     that I knew I'd have to tell.
Miss Dean was sorting Jack
     but that didn't turn her back.
Well that was a surprise...
     must have seen it in my eyes.
When no-one was about
     it just kind of tumbled out...
When, how, what
     and some old stuff I'd forgot.

I begged her not to tell...
     that part didn't go so well.
She thanked me for my trust
     but pass it on she must.
It kind of caused a jolt
     when she said it's not my fault.
And she stayed right by my side
     as I tumbled down the slide.
So now I'm sitting here
     and my whole life seems so clear.
We're
     Safe
     Now
And just think...
It started off at school...
just walking to the hall.

<u>Right Here Next To You</u>

People wanna travel the world??
Well I'm here,
You see – 'allo!
Right next to you.
     Talk to me
I'll tell you
All
About it.

People wanna travel in time??
Well I'm four thousand years of history,
Right here
Next to you.

Go on, talk to me
I'll tell you
All
About it.

I'm Not Good At Anything

Melissa's marvellous at Maths,
Gallespie's great at games.
At science Sam's sensational,
But not as good as James.

And when it comes to Literacy,
Latisha leads the lot.
She always writes *rectangle* right,
And puts the *k* in *knot*.

So see these swarms of super-kids,
Prowl proudly round the school.
But I'm not good at anything,
Anything at all.

...Except for maybe meeting mice,
And teaching them to dance.
Or growling grunts of *'Yes I can!'*,
Through all mum's *'No you can't!*s.

Uh Oh

Uh oh, oh no!
Uh oh, no way!
I forgot it was PE today!

Uh oh, oh no!
Don't look this way!
I forgot it was PE today!

Oh look at them,
Without a care,
Why do they all just stand and stare?

Oh look at them,
Without a care!
Well *they* remembered their underwear!

Anger

She looked at me.
I looked at her.
She told her mates.
They started to stir.

> *One deep breath,*
> *Count to ten.*
> *Bit o' Time Out,*
> *Join 'em again.*

She ignored me.
I ignored her.
She told her mates.
They started to stir.

> *One deep breath,*
> *Count to ten.*
> *Bit o' Time Out,*
> *Join 'em again.*

She flicked some mud.
My heart turned black.
She pushed my arm.
I pushed her back.

> *One deep breath,*
> *Count to ten.*
> *Bit o' Time Out,*
> *Join 'em again.*

She laughed at my mum.
I dissed her dad.
She just wouldn't stop
Driving me mad.

Continued overleaf.../

One deep breath,
Count to ten.
Bit o' Time Out,
Join 'em again.

She
Just
Wouldn't stop...
Driving
Me
Mad!

      One deep breath,
      Count to ten.
      Bit o' Time Out,
      Join 'em again.

I scratched her face.
She tore my coat.
I had my hands,
Right on her throat.

      One deep breath,
      Count to ten.
      Bit o' Time Out,
      Join 'em again.

Dinner-lady saw me,
Sent me away.
To be on my own.
For the rest of the day.

      One deep breath,
      Count to ten.
      Bit o' Time Out,
      Join 'em again.

She saw me coming,
Told all her friends.
Now they're all staring.
I wish this would end!

> *One deep breath,*
> *Count to ten.*
> *Bit o' Time Out,*
> *Join 'em again.*

I said I'm sorry.
She said 'me too.'
I'm still in trouble,
But I know what to do...

> *One deep breath,*
> *Count to ten.*
> *Bit o' Time Out,*
> *Join 'em again.*

My Mum Yelled At Me This Morning

My mum yelled at me this morning.
Surely the day couldn't get any worse?
But it did.
Oh – it did.
And you know why?
Cos my mum yelled at me this morning.
How could things get worse?
Well they did.
They definitely did.
They said I looked grumpy.
I felt grumpy.
I poked James Cooper.
You know why?
My mum yelled at me this morning.
She didn't even kiss me goodbye.
I poked James Cooper.
Made him cry.
They said I looked grumpy.
I was.

Kiki

Sat up like a statue,
Pointy ears pricked.
When I needed a friend to talk to,
It was always you I picked.

If a mouse had ran right past us,
You'd not have dashed away.
Only when I'd shared my secrets,
Would you have gone to play.

Kiki with your purring,
My broken heart you'd mend.
A cat just like no other,
My bestest bestest friend.

Is It Me?

Friday's
Come around again.
Assembly time.
It's five past ten.

> *Is it me?*
> *Could it be?*
> *Never, ever, clever me.*

Waiting...
For my name to come.
Assembly time.
I nailed that sum!

> *Is it me?*
> *Wait and see.*
> *Never, ever, clever me.*

Waiting...
My lungs fit to burst,
Assembly time.
I came in first!

> *Is it me?*
> *Let it be!*
> *Never, ever, clever me.*

Lewis,
On the stage again.
Assembly time.
He stole my pen!

Is it me?
Soon maybe?
Never, ever, clever me.

Friday...
Come around again!
Assembly time.
It's my turn then.

Whatever Happened To The Lollipop Lady?

Bright yellow coat,
Smile on her face,
The lollipop lady stood,
Outside Jack's place.

We all wait to cross,
We're all crowding around.
The lollipop lady waits,
Till there's no sound.

And then she's off, quick,
With a jump and hop,
To the middle of the road,
Where she holds her sign– **STOP**.

And that's what they do,
All those cars wait.
As we walk past in twos and threes,
To the school gate.

But now things are different,
She's gone now you see.
There's nobody to help,
Jack, Jade and me.

We stop, look and listen,
Just like we've been told,
And wait for the cars to stop,
In the rain, wind and cold.

We're always so careful,
But it takes hours and hours.
The cars just don't stop for us,
We don't have her powers.

Whatever happened to the lollipop lady?
In the dark and in the light,
Stopping all the traffic,
And making everything right?

www.ingramcontent.com/pod-product-compliance
Lightning Source LLC
Chambersburg PA
CBHW021149020426
42331CB00005B/967